STRESS-BUSTING STRATEGIES FOR TEACHERS

How do I manage the pressures of teaching?

M. Nora
MAZZONE

Barbara J.
MIGLIONICO

 Alexandria, VA USA

Website: www.ascd.org
E-mail: books@ascd.org
www.ascdarias.org

Printed in the United States of America. Cover art © 2014 by ASCD. ASCD publications present a variety of viewpoints. The views expressed or implied in this book should not be interpreted as official positions of the Association.

ASCD LEARN TEACH LEAD® and ASCD ARIAS™ are trademarks owned by ASCD and may not be used without permission. All other referenced trademarks are the property of their respective owners.

PAPERBACK ISBN: 978-1-4166-1939-0   ASCD product #SF114071
Also available as an e-book (see Books in Print for the ISBNs).

Library of Congress Cataloging-in-Publication Data
Mazzone, M. Nora.
  Stress-busting strategies for teachers : how do I manage the pressures of teaching? / M. Nora Mazzone and Barbara J. Miglionico.
    pages cm
  Includes bibliographical references.
  ISBN 978-1-4166-1939-0 (pbk. : alk. paper) 1. Teachers--Job stress. 2. Teachers--Job stress--Prevention. I. Miglionico, Barbara J. II. Title.
  LB2840.2.M29 2014
  371.1001'9--dc23
                              2014016241

21 20 19 18 17 16 15 14   1 2 3 4 5 6 7 8 9 10

STRESS-BUSTING STRATEGIES FOR TEACHERS

How do I manage the pressures of teaching?

Want to earn a free ASCD Arias e-book?
Your opinion counts! Please take 2–3 minutes to give
us your feedback on this publication. All survey
respondents will be entered into a drawing to
win an ASCD Arias e-book.

Please visit
www.ascd.org/ariasfeedback

Thank you!

Understanding Stress

If you are like many of our colleagues, you always wanted to be a teacher. Why? Perhaps a teacher played a critical role in your academic success or helped you through a difficult personal time. Many of us were motivated to be a teacher to repay that kindness and enhance the lives of children. We envisioned a career filled with happy students and imagined watching them grow intellectually and emotionally as a result of the environment and instruction we provided. What most of us did not anticipate were the significant challenges and stresses that we would face in our professional and personal lives.

We have all read about good stress and bad stress. Good stress can enhance motivation and help us excel. Stress can help us with challenges related to our interactions with colleagues, parents, and students. Stress may be induced by certain deadlines or duties or may be generally related to the environment and culture of the school. No matter the cause, productive or good stress helps us focus on our goals and stay resilient.

Negative stress, however, is the kind of stress that threatens our well-being. Negative stress is detrimental to our mental and physical health, both of which affect overall wellness and professional performance. You can recognize the tipping point between good stress and bad stress by becoming more aware and adept at monitoring how your body and mind feel, work, and respond. Healthy teachers make good instructional decisions, are alert and poised on the job, and provide a climate in which students are happy and productive. For healthy teachers, education is a calling and a rewarding lifelong profession.

The Reality of Teacher Stress

Getting out of work by 3 p.m. Good vacations. Summers off. How could teaching be as stressful as careers in business, law, or dentistry? Although many people believe that teaching is an easy job, the challenges are well documented.

> Growing demands and declining resources in school systems, along with economic challenges faced by family members of employees and students, cause stress that not only adversely influences employee morale and health, but also has a cascading effect throughout the system. (Reeves, 2010, p. 40)

Teachers who lack critical feedback and who are not adequately supported leave teaching at alarming rates. Keigher and colleagues (2010) found that more than 26.5 percent leave teaching to pursue other occupations. And, according to the *MetLife Survey of the American Teacher: Challenges for School Leadership* (2013), teacher satisfaction has declined 23 percent since 2008 and a shocking 51 percent of teachers report feeling under great stress several days a week or more. Only 2 percent of teachers reported that they are not experiencing stress on the job.

The results from the MetLife survey verified the escalating dissatisfaction of teachers and linked that discontent to school conditions and stress. Other studies detail the extensive challenges that teachers face each day when they come to school, identifying student behavior, workload, and school climate as key variables (Collie, Shapka, & Perry, 2012; Gold, Smith, Hopper, Herne, Tansey, & Hulland, 2010).

Teachers experience professional stress from a long list of contributors, including

- Lack of resources
- Difficult parents
- Lack of acknowledgment for professional expertise and skill set
- Diverse student needs due to cultural experiences and performance gaps
- Poor behavior from students
- Negative colleagues
- Unrealistic accountability measures from federal and local administrations

If professionals outside the field of education fail to acknowledge the pressures that teachers feel, it is more critical that professionals in education recognize, acknowledge, and address our stressors.

Look around and you can easily identify the signs of stress in your colleagues. Teachers who are overwhelmed do not exhibit stamina, good morale, high self-efficacy, patience, or creativity. They are tired at the beginning of the day and at the end of the day and are often absent or tardy. Stressed teachers have trouble meeting deadlines and fall behind in daily tasks such as returning phone calls and e-mail messages. They complain that there are not enough hours in the day to get the work done and that they are pulled in multiple directions simultaneously.

How do you know if you are experiencing early signs of stress? On quick examination, you will find a lack of professional and personal balance. The line between work and home will become increasingly blurry and you will feel that more is to be done at the end of each day than you have accomplished. Your day will be spent playing catch up and worrying that you cannot meet the needs of your family. The signs of teacher stress are everywhere, but we often deny or ignore them until the impact is significant enough that there are noticeable performance deficiencies.

Rethinking Negative Stressors

What causes negative stress for one person can cause positive stress for another. For example, videotaping a lesson or principal's walkthrough can bring out the best or the worst qualities in teachers and students. We know that stress comes from what we think (mindset) and what we experience (conditions). We also know that these two factors are intricately entwined and how you react both behaviorally and verbally can have a lasting impact on students

(Dweck, 2006). Challenging work conditions cause emotional responses and those emotions establish a mindset that you bring to work each day. The opposite is equally true. Your mindset can make a difference in how you perceive your conditions. If you go to work filled with bad feelings, your mindset will help to create a negative atmosphere that may contribute to challenging work conditions.

Clearly conditions impact our mindset and our mindset impacts our conditions, and both can cause stress. Here's an example. Your school doesn't meet Adequate Yearly Progress. The superintendent leans on the principal to beef up literacy instruction and the principal mandates a change in literacy pedagogy. In order to demonstrate to the superintendent that gains are being made, teachers are required to collect and send assessment data to the principal each month. The teachers are outraged. They feel that the administration does not respect them as professionals, recognize their hard work, or care about anything other than test scores.

Think about what just happened. The stress of change—forcing the adoption of new pedagogy and the requirement to report assessment data monthly—caused the teachers to react with a negative mindset. The teachers perceived from the change that the administration only values test scores and lacks appreciation for practice. The reciprocal relationship between mindset and conditions cannot be ignored. We can learn to ameliorate that interaction.

How often do you sit in the faculty room and hear comments like these?

- I heard from the elementary schools that next year's 6th grade class is the lowest-performing cohort that we have had in a long time. How are we going to get them to pass the state tests?
- This new schedule is impossible. There is not enough time to get our lessons aligned to the CCSS across grade levels.
- We are constantly expected to do more with fewer resources.

All educators recognize that these statements reflect real conditions. Some student cohorts are needier because of gaps in the curriculum. Responsible teachers inherently want to see all students succeed, but many feel added pressure from the accountability measures that use student scores as a gauge for determining the success of both students and teachers. And, it's obvious that new schedules can throw off pacing and time management—and that resources are strained and less plentiful with imposed tax caps. We can't change those realities.

What we *can* do is to alter the way we speak about these conditions as we set the foundation for developing a more positive and open mindset. Consider the impact that the following statements would have on your colleagues.

- I heard from the elementary schools that next year's 6th grade class is the lowest-achieving cohort that we have had in a long time. It's making me think about what I can do now to get ready. Perhaps we can share ideas earlier than usual so that we can focus our efforts on where these students need the most support to get through the state tests.

- This new schedule is challenging and I am having trouble staying ahead in my planning. Does anyone want to work together on lesson alignment? Maybe we can meet briefly and work on one segment of the unit. I will bring snacks!
- We are constantly expected to do more with fewer resources, yet we need to get the job done at the same high level. I have ordered some great new materials, but I also have a ton of stuff that I haven't used. Why don't we have a materials swap?

The difference between the two sets of statements lies within the relationship between conditions and mindset, which we establish by how we choose to think and react. Yes, *choose*, because our thinking is within our control. The first set shows difficult conditions plus a negative mindset. The second set reflects the same difficult conditions, but is offset by a positive mindset. A positive mindset provides us with the opportunity to think creatively and work collaboratively to get to our goal: we will be successful and we will support one another along the way.

Words and attitudes are amazingly infectious. Altering our mindset—the way we think about and speak about the conditions—offers us the opportunity to establish a positive school environment without denying that we have real obstacles to overcome.

Outcomes of Teacher Stress

The most important factor in student learning is the teacher (RAND, 2012). Healthy educators are able to provide a nurturing environment in which students feel safe, happy, and academically successful. Teachers who are overwhelmed by poor working conditions establish similar environments for their students and resort to teaching to the test, demanding high levels of performance without proper support, and reprimanding students more than motivating them.

The reality is that teachers spend more waking hours with a child than most parents. Those same students are observant and can learn important life lessons about resilience and compassion from their teachers. They look up to their teachers and are intensely aware of their verbal and nonverbal cues. Unfortunately, not all teachers are supported enough to be positive role models and not all students choose to respond in an understanding or cooperative manner when they sense the instability of a primary adult. Feeling a teacher's angst, students often react in ways that invite negative feedback. A cycle of negative reinforcement quickly develops and interferes with the emotional connection and energy required for student learning.

The challenges of daily life in the classroom can affect us in many ways. The behaviors of our students and the nearly constant changes in curriculum, pedagogy, leadership, and expectations can provoke anxiety in the most masterful practitioners. The stressors we experience can serve to energize us or to weigh us down in ways that affect our physical, emotional, and intellectual performance. It is critical to pay attention to health because a teacher's compromised capacity has a significant impact on the most precious educational stakeholders—the students.

Physical. It's all about awareness. What we are aware of, we can do something about. So pause and ask yourself the following question: "Am I regularly experiencing any of the following signs of stress?"

- Muscle tension, including stiff neck, headaches, and backaches
- Poor sleep
- Lack of stamina
- Frequent colds or feelings of illness
- Trouble with digestion or stomachaches
- Rapid breathing
- Elevated blood pressure
- Change in appetite

Stop and think about the ramifications. If a teacher cannot cope with the challenges of the work environment in a healthy way, she is more apt to neglect professional responsibilities, engage in negative or ineffective communication, become impatient with the energy and productive chatter of students, be absent more often, and have low professional confidence. As a result, supervisors exert more pressure to improve performance and the stress increases. It's a vicious cycle until it can be recognized and the teacher can actively employ strategies to help keep balanced or work toward rebalance.

Emotional. A stressed teacher experiences an over-abundance of emotion in response to the challenges of the day. The smallest misstep can evoke extreme irritation, anxiety, or even anger. Sometimes, just going to work brings forth a level of agitation and frustration that is unwarranted by what's going on in the present moment. Sure, it's normal to wish for the occasional snow day or to look forward to an upcoming break, but when Sunday nights are more about dreading Monday morning than enjoying popcorn and a movie with your family and friends, you should be suspicious that something is going askew.

Do you wake up in the middle of the night with a sense of nervous energy? Does your To Do list revolve and evolve in your mind and prevent you from going back to sleep? Do you find yourself feeling overwhelmed by being behind in paperwork and doing just enough to survive? Or wondering how to deal with Johnny's escalating poor behavior? Both anxiety and depression affect our ability to stay focused and alert during the school day. Teachers who feel stressed are more likely than their counterparts to be negative on the job, have higher incidents of classroom management problems, be impervious to feedback about their performance, be resentful of change, and be focused on their work and contractual issues more than the pleasures that come from teaching each day.

Intellectual. Even a cold can make us feel sluggish and scattered and compromise our intellectual capacity. Teaching is an intellectually rigorous and demanding profession.

Effective teachers need to be insatiably curious, astute, and creative. When doing our job well, we inspire children to learn more and to be resilient in the mastery of new knowledge. Teachers use keen observation and assessment skills to determine what each child needs to move him forward. We must expand our professional repertoire to address the diversity and accountability in today's school environment.

Using Stress-Busting Strategies

The work of a classroom teacher takes intelligence, alertness, and stamina. When the level of stress becomes too high, we notice less, forget more, demonstrate unclear thinking which impacts efficient planning and delivery of instruction, and have lapses in mental stamina affecting our ability to think quickly for long periods of time. The challenges in the educational environment are real. Veterans and new teachers need to be proactive in understanding and managing the stresses inherent in the profession. The strategies we provide can help you to increase your awareness and take control of your reactions and responses so that you can look forward to entering the classroom each day.

Responding to Stressful Situations

So what can you do to interrupt the cycle of negative stress? Start by building a foundation of awareness. Learn to identify the reactions and strategies that avert or deter negative stressors. After that, you can apply these behaviors to your professional and personal life and maintain a positive momentum throughout the school year. React, Generalize, and Maintain is one effective way to respond to and counteract stress.

React: How do I cope in the moment?

Generalize: How can I use this coping strategy to be proactive and extend to other instances?

Maintain: How can I maintain strategies that promote my wellness in and out of the classroom?

Nearly every decision affects our students and colleagues in specific ways. For example, if we don't frame a lesson objective clearly, students may be confused and their performance may be jeopardized.

It's the same with our emotional and behavioral actions. Have you ever entered a staff meeting in a good mood but exited in a bad mood because your colleagues spent the time complaining about a change in the schedule? Let's apply the React, Generalize, Maintain process to this scenario. In this case, we are trying to react to a negative mindset and prevent it from changing our overall feelings about the day.

React: How do I cope in the moment? First affirm. Tell your colleagues that you are also having trouble adapting to the new schedule and wonder if the group could share ideas that work well in the new structure. Talking about what has worked turns the conversation from a complaint session to a positive sharing experience.

Generalize: How can I use this coping strategy to be proactive and extend to other instances? You realize that when you asked colleagues for help, it provided them with a positive role. The focus changed the tone and tension level of the interaction almost immediately.

Maintain: Use the idea of asking others to help you overcome a problem and apply it whenever someone or a group is focusing on the negative aspects of a situation.

You can apply the same idea to a meeting with parents. For example, Mrs. Minton wants to meet about her son's math grade. You react defensively—in your experience, parents believe their children pay attention in class and do all their homework, so Mrs. Minton must think that you don't know how to teach. You feel nervous and wonder how you should respond and approach the meeting. Then you remember to use React, Generalize, and Maintain.

React: Can you draw on another experience that might help avert a negative meeting with the parent?

Generalize: You prepare for the meeting with information about her son's progress in math this year. You invite the math lab teacher and start the meeting by telling Mrs. Minton how excited you are to share information about her son's math skills and growth this year. Together with the lab teacher, show the diagnostic and formative data that indicate the learning objectives, gains made, and areas that need work. Then, ask Mrs. Minton to share what works when she is helping her son with homework. Mrs. Minton perks up and tells you about their homework routine and how her support has helped him complete the nightly assignments. You affirm her efforts and make some additional suggestions.

Maintain: You invite Mrs. Minton to communicate with you regularly. She leaves smiling and feeling that a new partnership has been established. You turned what could have been a negative interaction into a positive working relationship.

How has this experience added to your wellness? Consider the alternative. Mrs. Minton appears at the meeting with an armload of her son's work. She sits down and you thank her for coming in and ask her to explain her concerns. Mrs. Minton goes on a tirade, pulling out papers, talking about messy handwriting, and stating that her son just "doesn't get it." She demands to know what you are going to do about his lack of progress. You try best as you can to fend off her complaints, but in the end you are just glad that the meeting is over.

Your next class starts immediately and you can't help being tense and anxious. You wonder if Mrs. Minton stopped at the principal's office to complain or if she sent an e-mail message to the superintendent. You are preoccupied all day by what you could have said and are fearful of what will happen next. By the end of the day you are exhausted and just glad to go home. Your tension spills over from school and you are impatient with your family. Then you toss and turn and are deprived of a good night's sleep, setting you up for another long day.

Stop! Every aspect of your day and evening was disrupted because Mrs. Minton was negative. Using what you know from the discussion in the faculty room, you have the capacity to change the meeting tone and most likely save your entire day and evening. Not to mention averting a physical reaction to the stress. So maintain that positive tone and always strive to shift the direction of negative conversations. It works!

Remember, each reaction has an antecedent and a consequence for ourselves and those around us. More times than not, the consequence is stress or a feeling of things being out of control in the work environment. Therefore, we must closely consider our reactions to things and people around us because we have the power to turn negative stressors into positive events. So stop and think before you react. And ask yourself what you can do to turn a negative situation into a positive one.

Try it! And then notice what happens. Make a mental note and then do it again another time. Continuing this type of behavior will maintain your professional self-efficacy, confidence, and personal health.

Know Yourself and What You Need

Lesson plans, curriculum alignment, individual education plans, e-mail messages, differentiated materials, parent phone calls, and child study team meetings. These are just some of the daily responsibilities of classroom teachers and it sometimes feels like you have to do them simultaneously.

Do people forget that your primary job is to manage a classroom full of students?

To meet your responsibilities, determine what it is that you need to do to work most effectively. When, where, and how do you get the most productive work done and what resources do you need? What is your professional pace? When do you work best? How long can you work without needing a break?

We all have peak periods in the day when the ideas flow and we work most effectively. It is important that you identify your peak periods and capitalize on those moments at every opportunity. Stress emerges when we feel pushed to perform too far outside our natural limits without taking time to reenergize ourselves. So know when you work best and when you need breaks to sustain high performance (Loehr & Schwartz, 2003). If you know that you work best in the early morning, get yourself to school before everyone arrives and do your heaviest brain work then. Although most teaching schedules include a dedicated planning period, that doesn't mean your hardest work has to be done when your body and mind would be best doing something of a less rigorous nature. Likewise, if you aren't productive at night, don't try to bang out your lessons before going to bed. You are sure to be sluggish and to take twice as long to complete them.

Teaching requires both stamina and focus. Self-regulation is as important for a teacher as it is for an athlete. Our environment, actions, attitudes, habits, and diet all contribute to building stamina and calmness in the work day. Ask and address the following questions.

- **Where and with whom do I work most effectively?**
We all have preferences when it comes to getting work done. Some teachers prefer to collaborate on lesson plans and are energized by having colleagues around them. Other teachers find planning together an extremely stressful endeavor because it requires depending on others to do their part, debating ideas, and using strategies that are incompatible with their teaching strengths (Collie, Shapka, & Perry, 2012). Also, consider environmental factors. Avoid cluttered work spaces, as they lead to lost time and anxiety from searching for items that you need to get the job done. Know whether you need quiet or background music or noise. Plan where and with whom you can work the best. It's part of your own professional self-advocacy.

- **In what areas do I need support?** Practitioners must be broadly conversant to get the job done. The increasing diversity of demographics demands that we constantly expand our professional toolboxes. Stay abreast of new educational trends to avoid the stress of playing catch up or being compared to colleagues who are more informed. As the job of teacher rapidly evolves, we must acknowledge where we need support. It is not acceptable to do the job the same way as a decade ago. For example, not long ago it was the responsibility of middle school English teachers to teach reading and writing in those grades. Not anymore. The Common Core now requires all teachers to incorporate literacy skills and to teach all students how to digest large amounts of informational text and make complex cognitive connections. As our profession changes, we must seek the supports we need to transform our approach to teaching and learning. Don't be afraid to ask for what you need to add to your instructional repertoire—you will earn respect for your desire to grow.

• **How do I learn best? Who or what can provide needed resources?** Without continuous growth, you will be unable to meet the extensive set of demands coming your way as an educator. Do something to expand your practice and self-efficacy. Join professional associations, online discussion groups, or seek a knowledgeable colleague. Don't hesitate to search for resources or ask for support in finding them. Comfortable professional growth occurs when the resources are well-matched to your learning style. Don't wait for someone to tell you that change or growth needs to happen, be your own advocate. The "I will wait until they tell me what they want" approach, although easy, will most certainly cause the type of stress that you want to avoid.

Fuel the Day

It's 8 a.m. Mrs. Jamison quickly pulls out the materials for period 1. As her algebra students enter the room, she logs on to take attendance. The classroom phone rings. Mr. James, the 9th grade counselor, asks if he can stop by to collect the homework assignment that Emily missed last week.

Emily's mother is stopping by on her way to work, so Mrs. Jamison pulls materials together as she reminds students that there is a test on Friday. Hands pop up and she attempts to respond to questions while she finishes taking attendance. This is early in period 1. Looking ahead at the day, Mrs. Jamison will teach five different levels of math classes, meet with the Committee on Special Education during her planning period, post the night's homework, and serve as the "extra help" math teacher during lunch.

Prepare yourself for a successful day by fueling your body with the proper nutrients and keeping it adequately hydrated. As teachers, we work hard to take care of our students, sometimes at great detriment to ourselves. Taking the time to balance what we eat and drink throughout the school day can nurture our ability to stay calm and focused from morning to night. Teachers make thousands of spontaneous decisions throughout the school day, so we must be at our best for the best to happen.

Coffee isn't the only important drink in your morning. Have a large glass of water with lemon. Coffee dehydrates your body and will zap your body of energy, but the water will help you sustain alertness throughout the morning. The lemon helps to flush the toxins that have settled in through the night. Although advertising in the media touts orange juice as a morning drink, most juices have added sugar that pumps you and lets you down. Your breakfast should include a complex carbohydrate to raise your serotonin level, assuring that the day begins with patience and fortitude. If you eat or drink dairy products, they can be a good option because they contain tryptophan to regulate your mood. Fruit is also important. Bananas, strawberries, oranges, blueberries, kiwis, and apples have the most rewarding nutrients. Fruits are best when eaten alone because it is the easiest way for our bodies to process the sugar, fiber, and nutrients. However, fruit is a great pick-me-up and is good as a snack or part of a meal.

Midmorning snacks are routine in elementary schools and are useful in secondary schools to supplement energy before a late lunch or after an early one. Keep raw almonds in your desk or carry baby carrots or other small pieces of raw vegetables in an insulated lunch bag. Make every effort to stay away from simple carbs such as crackers and chips. Although they are tempting and packaged to go, the immediate sugar rush is deceiving.

Take time to pack your own lunch to avoid the salt, preservatives, and additives in prepared foods. A sandwich made with whole grain bread or lettuce wrap and lean proteins such as chicken, turkey, or fish will keep you satisfied until dinner. Cottage cheese or a kale and spinach salad are also good choices. The vitamin C in kale and spinach will help build up your immune system to fight germs from your students and colleagues. An extra piece of fruit for the end of the day can give you energy for family errands or the gym.

Don't let down when you get home. Remember the old adage: garbage in, garbage out. Red meat slows your digestion, resulting in feeling more sluggish than usual in the morning. Although that extra glass of wine might ensure that you fall asleep quickly, without enough water you will be foggy and lack a clear head to react to the pressures of the next day. Good options for dinner include chicken, turkey, wild salmon or cod, and beans. Be sure to add onion and garlic. The tryptophan and B6 in these foods will calm you and help you get the night's sleep required for recharging and refreshing your mind and body. If you enjoy eating something after dinner, try popcorn (no butter or salt) or nuts with a cup of chamomile tea. These simple changes will give you a peaceful beginning to the next day.

If you want help getting started on fueling for success, see Resources for three days of meal suggestions. The main thing to remember is that you should balance protein, fats, carbohydrates, and hydration. Try to distribute them proportionately throughout the day and your mood will improve and you will have more patience in the classroom.

Set Goals for Work and Life Balance

Take stock of your life and set two goals that will make you feel better about yourself and your work. Try setting one personal goal and one professional goal. Why? We are at our best when we feel that there is balance between our professional and personal obligations. Therefore, it's most productive to set goals that push us forward in both areas.

If any of the following statements sound familiar, your life and goals may not be as balanced as you think.

- Weekends are primarily viewed as a time to catch up on what you couldn't get done during the work week.
- Days off from school are just as hectic and scheduled as when you are in the building.

- Social gatherings are less frequent because you would rather stay home and get some rest.
- You have no time to do anything well.

Here are examples of goals to help you get started with ideas that can make a difference in your life.

- **Professional.** I will join a professional organization and read the resources that are part of my membership. From those materials, I will find new research-based ideas to use in my classroom.
- **Professional.** I will reorganize the reading corner so that students find it inviting and useful. Students will be able to easily select books which may increase their overall reading.
- **Professional.** I will reserve 20 minutes each day to communicate with parents. If I am diligent about answering e-mail messages in a timely manner, parents will view me as responsive and caring.
- **Professional.** I will develop a classroom web page to keep parents and students aware of assignments and expectations. A web page will enable parents to support their children and will reduce the number of e-mail messages regarding homework and projects.
- **Personal.** I will self-assess my stress level and identify one relaxation exercise to try at the end of each day.
- **Personal.** I will set up a personal exercise routine that feels manageable.
- **Personal.** I will plan at least three healthy dinners for the week instead of waiting until I get home and

making do with whatever is fastest or picking up food on the way home.

Take stock of your goals every three months. If your goals no longer feel like a stretch for you, try revising them and push yourself to the next level. But remember, too fast and too much may cause stress, so be kind to yourself when starting out. Even the smallest amount of progress is worthwhile and should be celebrated.

Prioritize To-Do Lists

You can do only so much in one day. Teaching requires continuous, spontaneous human interactions. Therefore, when you are bombarded by the needs of multiple students and adults each day, it is all too easy to get swept up and lose focus of what you need to get done. Not everything is equally urgent. If you try to do it all, you will be exerting self-induced pressure that will backfire. Avoid getting to the end of the day and realizing that your To Do list has multiplied. Try this morning tip. Start each morning with a 3+ List. The three tasks are your nonnegotiable tasks that will make the day feel productive and successful. Rank them. Then add two "plus" tasks. Your plus tasks are not urgent and can be considered bonuses if you actually get to them. When you get to work, post the 3+ List where you will see it often and cross off each item as you get it done.

Monday's 3+ List

1. Create tiered math assignment for tomorrow night's homework.

2. Organize homogeneous book club groups.

3. Send an e-mail blast to parents about an upcoming field trip.

Plus List

+1. Arrange a time to meet with the literacy coach next week.

+2. Request whiteboard markers and masking tape.

Stay attentive to your three tasks during the school day and don't add to them. After crossing off those tasks, you can consider working on the plus tasks. Plus tasks eventually make their way to the top of the list unless they are achieved as pluses.

Manage Time

Life in a school is dictated by the clock. We are often pacing a lesson, waiting for the bell to ring, or judging how long students can work independently before a class management concern erupts. Here are some strategies to take control of your time before it takes control of you.

- Establish a calendar with deadlines set up for important or time-consuming tasks to avoid the anxiety of a last-minute rush. Work backward and document interim deadlines. Breaking up bigger tasks makes them less stressful and you will be less apt to make mistakes, typos, or errors of omission. And it will feel good to have the tasks done on time.

- Consider the cycles of your workflow. One of the best things about teaching is the cyclical nature of the school year. The fall requires us to think about old routines and how to make them better with new students. The winter is heavy with new content. Spring represents the last leg, time to play catch up and wrap up. Each cycle demands time and attention. Use your experience to anticipate what that means for you and the time you need to prepare. Plan ahead so that you will feel more in control and less pressure. You might even have some free time on your hands!

- Plan for downtime. If you don't plan for it, it might not happen. Downtime doesn't refer to just time after work. Take dedicated breaks during the day. Find a conflict-free environment to relax or eat stress-reducing foods. Downtime is a lost opportunity for recharging if it is spent around people who are complaining. Surround yourself with the people who feed your professional soul or spend a few quiet moments alone. If you can fit it in, walk around the building. You will be amazed at the effect downtime can have on your stamina and attitude throughout the rest of the day.

If one of your personal goals is to exercise, pursue a hobby, or spend high-quality time with family, you have to schedule the time. Many teachers volunteer for committees and take on extracurricular responsibilities beyond contractual obligations. It is wonderful to be involved in the life of the school community, but beware of overbooking. Once you are past your personal threshold for time and energy spent, you have compromised your productivity and will require even more downtime to bring yourself back into balance. Schedule downtime as you would any important event in your life. Start with a few times a week and then see if you can extend it to a daily dose for your own health.

- Digitize whenever possible. Don't waste time by handwriting lessons and materials only to recreate them later. Use technology to your benefit. Digitize your plans, materials, and instructional displays. It will make revisions much easier and ensure materials are in a readily accessible place, whether you are at home or at school.

- Take a second look at how you spend time. If you are using these strategies to save time yet there's still not enough time in the day, revisit how you spend your time. Keep a list or log of how you spend the next 24–48 hours and note what activities took up large portions of your time. See if there are any patterns so that you can learn from the data. Often this type of reflection reveals that we spend inordinate amounts of time on tasks from which there is minimal value-added.

Delegate Tasks

How many times have you stayed late to clean up, put away stray items, rearrange furniture, or go through piles of notes? Most of us would say too many times. We use precious time to do mundane tasks that help things look and feel nice, but aren't at the core of what we need to do. And then we become tense because we never finished responding to e-mail messages or lesson planning and it's time to go home. The less critical classroom tasks should be done but you don't have to be the one to do them. You can delegate them as part of the classroom routine.

- Get your students onboard. Start and end the day with 5 minutes of housekeeping tasks. Students can set up and collate materials, put away belongings, monitor clean-up of workspaces, collect and distribute materials, and adapt desk arrangements. If you explicitly delineate what each job involves, students will take them on with pride and save you precious time.
- Use interns, parents, and community volunteers— as allowed by your school's policies. Often, we can capture precious time to confer with a student or meet with a small group if an adult volunteer is there to help.
- Ask colleagues for help. If you hesitate to ask, try offering to help a colleague with a simple task. If you are going to the copy room, see if the neighboring teacher has anything to drop off. Going to the supply room to pick up pencils? Maybe the teacher down the hall needs pencils, too. Little kindnesses can make teaching colleagues feel supported and more likely to reciprocate.

Set Parameters

Students learn how to regulate their time and behaviors through guidelines and parameters that the teacher models and establishes for them. Teachers who have solid management skills set up guidelines, structures, and deadlines that empower students. Truly effective teachers consciously set limits and parameters that enable both learner and practitioner to work comfortably and successfully.

Get Organized

Some days it makes sense to leave school at 3 p.m. to fit in a trip to the gym, other days an extra 20 minutes of planning and organizing makes more sense. If you are organized, you can use instructional time efficiently and offer transparency of learning objectives, strategies, and routines. Organization leads to a sense of control which in turn enhances your sense of well-being and self-confidence.

Being organized requires routines and learning structures that will make the most of classroom time. Use these tools to avoid disruption during instructional time:

- Trays or folders near the door with materials relevant to the day's lesson. Students can pick up the materials as they enter.
- Tray for notes and materials that students may have missed during a recent absence.
- Message center where you can post sealed reminder notes for individual students. Message centers can take many different forms, both digital and traditional. For example, you may choose bulletin boards, easels, e-mail messages, or a digitally secure forum to protect the privacy of students.

- Bins marked for different genres of books, discipline-specific materials, or other categories of resources that facilitate students' abilities to find appropriate materials.
- Charts that detail steps of a learning task, process, or project (e.g., steps of the inquiry process or fix-up strategies to support independent reading time).
- Standard place to post learning objectives, homework assignments, and announcements of tasks. If students know the learning objective and expectations, they will be better equipped to be active participants in their own learning.
- List of activities for "when you are done" tasks. Learners need to know what they are expected to do if they finish an assigned task earlier than their peers. Provide and discuss a list of acceptable options.
- List of student roles and responsibilities that help to keep the classroom well-groomed and functional throughout the day. Even secondary students require dedicated material organization and clean-up routines.

A cluttered, disorganized classroom is often a reflection of an unprepared and overwhelmed teacher. In fact, clutter can add to the feeling of being overwhelmed for some people. Practitioners who are on top of the instructional game are less stressed, more confident, and able to be more flexible and responsive in the classroom.

Adopt a Positive Mindset

Are you a positive person? Would colleagues describe you as having a positive attitude at work? Positive people are happy, despite the challenges they face. Some of the healthiest work climates develop when colleagues work extremely hard toward a common goal. A positive environment or attitude is not dependent on how many students complete the homework assignment or the percentage of English language arts scores in the mastery range. The common goal of teaching is student learning. So why do we struggle so much to stay positive? Teachers who are positive are more productive, effective, and energetic.

We don't always recognize that we are being negative. Ask yourself the following questions:

- Do I look forward to coming to work after a weekend or vacation?
- Do I feel like there are things that I do well? Can I name them?
- Do I feel like I am making a difference in the classroom?

If you answered yes to these quesstions, then you are a positive force in the work environment to whom others gravitate. If not, then you need to focus on developing a positive mindset. When you go to work this week, commit to some of the following behaviors and see if you notice a difference in the way you feel and in how others respond to you.

- Say good morning or hello first

- Smile and listen carefully to your colleagues
- Replace the phrase "I can't" with "I can" when responding to requests. For example, "I can help plan for our presentation on Monday, but I need to keep Tuesday open to update my class web page." Consciously starting with "I can . . ." will enable you to graciously and professionally avoid overcommitment.
- Respond professionally and respectfully no matter what (or who) is coming your way
- Stop griping
- Identify one thing you do well each day
- Identify one thing that went well during your day
- Name one person you enjoy working with and why

Turn off the negative noise that has been playing in your head. Sometimes just acting positive can change the way we feel. Don't add to your own stress by engaging in negative behaviors. Be a positive and productive member of the school community.

Establish Strong Communication Skills and Relationships

Communication and relationships are at the heart of teaching. Armed with good communication skills, teachers can deliver instruction with the clarity and explicitness that students need. Understanding what a teacher expects is an opportunity for students to cultivate positive interactions with their teacher.

Students thrive when they feel connected to a significant adult in the school community—most of the time, this adult is their classroom teacher. Both adults and students are inclined to work hard when they have established a good relationship with one another, as well as with others in the broader school environment. What is the quality of your relationships with students, parents, administrators, and other staff? Do you communicate easily and productively with those around you? Are there differences in how you communicate when you feel defensive, overwhelmed, or generally stressed?

Here are some proven communication tips that can help you establish and maintain good relationships.

- Stay open and take communication from others at face value. Much of the conflict in the course of our workday is a result of us deciding what someone meant long after the conversation ended. Spare yourself angst and either go back and clarify with the person or take the words at face value.

- Respond thoughtfully. Good communication comes more out of listening than reacting.

- Always affirm. Indicate to students and colleagues that you understand the message or circumstances that they are trying to relay. Don't rush to make suggestions or solve problems for them.

- Establish oral and written communication parameters that are responsive and comfortable. E-mail is a dangerous communication medium for sensitive or confidential messages. If you receive a potentially upsetting e-mail message from a parent or colleague, think twice before shooting off a reply. It is often more effective to walk down the hall or to pick up the phone. When talking in person, you have the opportunity to use gesture, inflection, and expression to convey your intended meaning. Even a phone conversation allows immediate two-way communication and vocal inflections to clarify misconceptions.

You cannot be happy and productive without positive working relationships with your colleagues in the hallways, classrooms, offices, and lounge. Being approachable, thoughtful, and affirming will enable you to have solid working relationships with everyone, even with those whose philosophies or practices differ from yours. It is also important to establish a group of trusted colleagues who can serve as critical friends when you do need an outlet or help to think outside the box.

Nutrition Counts

When stressed, we can be drawn to what we perceive as comfort food. Unfortunately, these foods do not always represent the best choices. It is time to change the definition of comfort foods! Comfort foods should be foods that make your body comfortable. These are the real foods that increase your serotonin level and boost your immune system. The intake of these foods results in decreasing cortisol levels in your body, lowering blood pressure, and controlling weight gain. When we consume foods that increase our physical comfort, it puts both our body and mind at ease. Here are some basic ideas that can help you get started on a healthier nutrition plan.

- Drink more tea than coffee. Coffee causes adrenalin to shoot up, which in turn raises cortisol and blood pressure. Black tea is a far healthier alternative to coffee.
- Choose foods high in vitamin C to lower stress levels and blood pressure.
- Eat healthy fats such as those found in nuts, avocado, and salmon. We all need good fat in our diet and these are full of omega-3s. They will reduce inflammation in your body and keep you well. In general, vitamin E helps to fight disease-causing free radicals and magnesium in avocados lowers your blood pressure. Avocados are also high in heart-healthy good fats, known as monounsaturated fats.
- Pack a stress-busting lunch (see Food for Stress Relief).
- Avoid red meat and choose lean proteins, plenty of leafy greens, beans, and legumes for dinner. The magnesium will help you sleep and vitamin B will help calm and maintain a healthy nervous system.
- Increase serotonin/tryptophan levels by consuming complex carbohydrates in the evening.
- Avoid nicotine, caffeine, excessive alcohol, sugar, hydrogenated oils, and high-fructose corn syrup. Many of these ingredients are found in soda, juice, condiments, and fast foods.

- Review the three days of simple meal suggestions in Resources. A special salad recipe with nutrients sure to alleviate stress at any time of the day is also included.

It is not only what you eat that makes your body comfortable, but also where and how. Avoid eating in unhealthy conditions. If the conversation in the faculty room is negative or causes stress, move to a place that is more peaceful. Likewise, don't let paperwork and phone calls accompany your lunch. Sit and enjoy. Meal times are to help you reenergize physically and mentally.

Engage in Physical Exercise

The big idea behind exercise as a stress-buster is to increase oxygen to the brain and lower your stress level. Include both aerobic and anaerobic exercise. The benefit of aerobic exercises—walking, running, or dancing—is that they increase oxygen to the brain which makes you alert and focused. Anaerobic exercises, such as using weights or doing crunches, release stress through effort applied. If you cannot find the time, shorter stints offer benefits. Again, remember that it is best to start slowly. Aim to exercise 30 minutes a day at first. Any additional time or effort devoted to exercise can improve your health and how you feel.

We all have those days when we get into the car at the end of the day and think "What a day. I am too tired to go to the gym. I am just going to go home and relax." Fight that response. Forcing yourself to maintain an exercise routine is in your best interest and will make you less tired and stressed the next day (Parker-Pope, 2008). Stick with it! Join a gym that is on your way home and you will be more apt to stop for a short workout than if the location is inconvenient.

Create Mindfulness

When we incorporate mental exercises into our daily routine, we train our minds to stay focused on what's most important and not to be distracted by insecurities and anticipation. A prime example is the extreme stress that teachers experience in relation to standardized testing: "How am I going to get everyone into the passing range? What will happen if I don't?" With these underlying worries, it's no wonder that teachers feel distracted and overwhelmed.

What kind of calming routines (mental exercise) can nurture mindfulness? There are many, but here are several you can start with.

- **Basic meditation.** Sit in a quiet place and focus on taking slow, deep breaths to a count of five. As with any exercise, start with short intervals and gradually increase the time you meditate. Try to capture a few minutes during the workday for meditation and notice the difference in how you feel. At home, you may choose to light a candle and concentrate on the flame while repeating the sound "OM," using a favorite mantra, or listening to music. Remember to concentrate on your breathing.
- **Visualization.** Think of a special place or time and just let your mind "be there."

- **Breathing exercise.** Close your eyes and breathe in deeply through your nose as you count slowly to 5. Exhale slowly through your mouth while counting from 5 to 8. Keep your breathing slow and controlled for several minutes prior to entering a stressful meeting or starting the school day. You may use this technique at the end of the workday and before going to bed.
- **Mantra.** Identify a positive mantra, such as "Today I want to be someone I would choose as my friend." Repeat it a minimum of three times; use more repetitions if that helps to soothe you. Try it with your students at the start of the day or after recess to bring them into a calm, present focus.
- **Yoga.** Performing yoga poses, arm stretches, leg stretches, and neck stretches can help you feel better overall, increase your flexibility, prevent injury, and move around desks and crowded hallways with ease.
- **Tai Chi.** Try this meditative physical exercise for relaxation and improved balance.
- **Aromatherapy.** Explore the use of soothing, calming scents such as lavender, peppermint, eucalyptus, and bergamot. Candles, diffusers, lotions, and sprays with your favorite scents are among options.
- **Spiritual health.** Find your spirit to feel your spirit! To be on your way to total wellness, take ownership of your spiritual health (traditional or nontraditional) to enjoy whole health and a well self.

Conclusion

Stress within the teaching profession has a negative impact on the health and well-being of individual teachers and on retention and recruitment for the profession as a whole. (Gold et al., 2009, p. 184)

If you are struggling to manage the daily challenges of being a teacher, it's time to get to work on your wellness. Treating your symptoms after a stressful day in the classroom will only work for so long. Start small by answering the self-assessment questions in the Encore section and using that information to choose a few of the stress-busting strategies that will help you feel more comfortable, productive, and in control. If you notice the benefits of the changes you make, you will be motivated to try other strategies that can increase your personal and professional health.

To prevent burnout, adopt new routines and a healthy diet that are sustainable, use physical and mental exercises to help keep your life in balance, set goals that are achievable and realistic, and try out different strategies that can act as a guide through difficult situations. Keep yourself healthy so that you teach to your best ability and feel good while you are doing it.

A teacher makes all the difference.

To give your feedback on this publication and
be entered into a drawing for a free ASCD
Arias e-book, please visit
www.ascd.org/ariasfeedback

ASCD | arias™

ENCORE

STRESS SELF-ASSESSMENT

1. Do you feel productive and have a sense of accomplishment at the end of the day?

2. Do you feel well organized?

3. Do you sleep well?

4. Do you pay attention to the nutritional value of what you eat more than the calories?

5. Do you feel that you are balancing your professional and personal obligations?

6. Do you feel highly competent and successful?

7. Do you enjoy spending time with your colleagues each day?

8. Do you enjoy your job and look forward to going to work?

9. Do you exercise regularly?

10. Do you engage in relaxation exercises for body and mind?

If you answered "no" to more than three of these questions, you need to make an effort to remove stress from your life. Choose two concepts to work on (perhaps one personal and one professional) that address your weakest areas.

SUGGESTIONS FOR

THREE DAYS OF HEALTHY EATING

Day 1 Breakfast
Oatmeal with flax seeds and almond milk
Banana
Coffee
Water

Day 1 Lunch
Turkey wrapped with sprouted grain bread or
    lettuce and a few kale leaves
Cucumber or baby carrots
Water with lemon slice

Day 1 Dinner
Wild salmon on raw arugula
Asparagus
Quinoa
Water

Day 2 Breakfast
Yogurt with almonds or walnuts
Berries
Tea
Water

Day 2 Lunch
Mixed green salad with garbanzo beans and tomatoes
Olive oil and balsamic vinegar dressing
Apple with almond butter
Water

Day 2 Dinner
Baked chicken breast
Kale sautéed in coconut or olive oil
Baked sweet potato
Water with lemon slice

Day 3 Breakfast
Eggs
Toast with flax oil
Coffee
Water

Day 3 Lunch
Cottage cheese with flax, chia, or sesame seeds
Celery
Pear
Water

Day 3 Dinner
Lentils and potatoes
Arugula salad
Water with lemon slice

Spinach, Sunflower Seed, and Strawberry Salad

5   oz. baby spinach

¼   cup toasted sunflower seeds

3   oz. goat cheese, crumbled

Strawberry vinaigrette dressing

5   strawberries

1   tablespoon balsamic vinegar

1   tablespoon fresh lemon juice

4   tablespoons olive oil

1   teaspoon honey (optional)

½   teaspoon sea salt

1   small garlic clove, minced

5–7 basil leaves (fresh)

1   tablespoon red onion or shallot (minced or chopped)

Black pepper, to taste

Directions

1. Put the spinach and sunflower seeds in a bowl. Set aside.

2. In a blender or food processor, blend dressing ingredients until emulsified. Add black pepper to taste.

3. Drizzle the dressing over the spinach and sunflower seeds and toss.

4. Garnish with goat cheese.

Refrigerate the extra dressing for up to a week.

References

Collie, R. J., Shapka, J. D., & Perry, N. E. (2012). School climate and social-emotional learning: Predicting teacher stress, job satisfaction, and teaching efficacy. *Journal of Educational Psychology, 104*(4), 1189-1204.

Dweck, C. (2006). *Mindset: The new psychology of success.* New York: Ballantine Books.

Gold, E., Smith, A., Hopper, I., Herne, D., Tansey, G., & Hulland, C. (2010). Mindfulness-based stress reduction (mbsr) for primary school teachers. *Journal of Child and Family Studies, 19*(2), 184-189.

Keigher, A. (2010). *Teacher attrition and mobility: Results from the 2008–09 teacher follow-up survey* (NCES 2010-353). U.S. Department of Education. Washington, DC: National Center for Education Statistics. Retrieved May 12, 2014, from http://nces.ed.gov/pubsearch

Loehr, J., & Schwartz, T. (2003). *The power of full engagement: Managing energy, not time, is the key to high performance and personal renewal.* New York: Free Press.

MetLife survey of the American teacher: Challenges for school leadership. (February, 2013). Retrieved from https://www.metlife.com/assets/cao/foundation/MetLife-Teacher-Survey-2012.pdf

Parker-Pope, T. (2008, February 29). The cure for exhaustion: More exercise. *New York Times.* Retrieved from http://well.blogs.nytimes.com/2008/02/29/the-cure-for-exhaustion-more-exercise/?_php=true&_type=blogs&_r=0

RAND Education. (2012). Teachers matter: Understanding teachers' impact on student achievement. Retrieved from www.rand.org/education/projects/measuring-teacher-effectiveness/teachers-matter.html

Reeves, D. (2010). Dealing with stress and anxiety. *American School Board Journal, 197*(2), 40-41.

Resources

The following websites are some of our favorites that support reflection and growth.

Culinary Nutrition
MW Culinary Wellness: www.martiwolfson.com

Healthy Living
Everyday Health: www.everydayhealth.com

Professional Support for Educators
ASCD: www.ascd.org
Association for Middle Level Education: www.amle.org
Research for Better Teaching: www.rbteach.com
 /rbteach2/home.html

Recipes, Fitness, and Green Living
Wholeliving: www.wholeliving.com

Words of Wisdom and Encouragement
Daily Love: www.thedailylove.com

Related Resources

At the time of publication, the following ASCD resources were available (ASCD stock numbers appear in parentheses). For up-to-date information about ASCD resources, go to www.ascd.org. You can search the complete archives of *Educational Leadership* at http://www.ascd.org/el.

The Inspired Teacher: How to Know One, Grow One, or Be One by Carol Frederick Steele (#108051)

Motivating Students and Teachers in an Era of Standards by Richard Sagor (#103009)

The New Teacher's Companion: Practical Wisdom for Succeeding in the Classroom by Gini Cunningham (#109051)

Qualities of Effective Teachers, 2nd Edition by James H. Stronge (#104156)

The Well-Balanced Teacher: How to Work Smarter and Stay Sane Inside the Classroom and Out by Mike Anderson (#111004)

When Teaching Gets Tough: Smart Ways to Reclaim Your Game by Allen N. Mendler (#112004)

THE WHOLE CHILD The Whole Child Initiative helps schools and communities create learning environments that allow students to be healthy, safe, engaged, supported, and challenged. To learn more about other books and resources that relate to the whole child, visit www.wholechildeducation.org.

For more information: send e-mail to member@ascd.org; call 1-800-933-2723 or 703-578-9600, press 2; send a fax to 703-575-5400; or write to Information Services, ASCD, 1703 N. Beauregard St., Alexandria, VA 22311-1714 USA.

About the Authors

M. Nora Mazzone is a middle level school administrator in Mamaroneck, N.Y., and doctoral adjunct professor for Pace University. She has extensive experience in public education as a special education teacher, teacher leader, and school administrator. Mazzone has presented on the topics of leadership and stress management for ASCD. Her doctoral research explored the impact of student-generated feedback on teacher practice through the use of response system technology. Mazzone welcomes contact from readers and is available for workshops and consultations. She can be reached at dr.nmazzone@gmail.com.

Barbara J. Miglionico is the executive director of a school-age child care program in Westchester County, New York, and is a certified nutrition and wellness consultant through American Fitness Professionals and Associates. Miglionico has been educating people of all ages and all stages of life about health and well-being for 35 years. Her experiences include teaching physical education and health classes in public schools, youth summer fitness programs, college weight training classes, and senior center wellness groups. She is a member of several nutrition, wellness, and fitness professional organizations and enjoys sharing her lifelong passion. Miglionico has assisted individuals with creating

lifestyles to restore and maintain health, taught at health centers, and conducted nutrition seminars. She can be reached
at bjmiglionico@gmail.com.

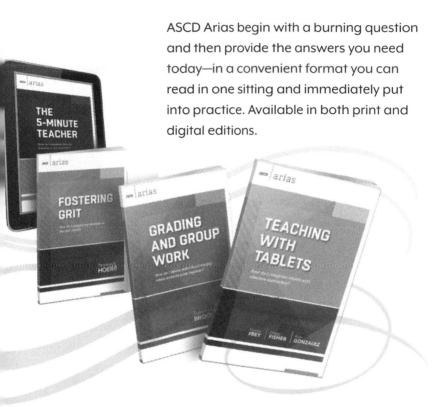